LOOKING BACK AT
NORTHENDEN
Derick Deakin

Willow
PUBLISHING

©Willow Publishing 1983
Willow Cottage, 36 Moss Lane,
Timperley, Altrincham,
Cheshire, WA15 6SZ.

ISBN 0 946361 03 7

Printed by The Commercial
Centre Ltd., Clowes Street,
Hollinwood, Oldham.

Acknowledgements

We would like to thank the many people who have given or loaned photographs and other matter and countless others for their help and good will. Please note that the copyright remains with the owner of the illustration.

Of the pictures we have been able to use we would like to note the following whose contributions have ranged from a score to single items. John Hill-Wilson for pictures throughout the book but especially in the later sections: Michael Saul, builder of Sale, through the mediation of David Mycock for the cache of pictures, (including the one of the Church Inn on the cover,)by Mr. Warren whose Cash Drug Store appears in the Church Road section; Douglas Howard for a variety of material especially on Leisure and Pleasure; Greg Forster, Rector, for use of pictures that have graced the parish magazine Concord; Rod Bladen, John Davies and Cultural Services for use of items from the Royle Collection and the Central Library; Lilywhite – Larkfield Printing – Post Cards, Barry Bettamy, Editor of the Stockport/Wythenshawe Express, Alan Smyllie for professional help and advice; Denis Thorpe and the Manchester Guardian for the flying-bus picture in the last section; and Ernest Anthony of the Methodist Church, Robert Armstrong, Barrow Motors, Gladys Barlow, Phyllis Bunn, Pete Brennan, Jack Close of the British Legion, Les Davies, Frank Freeman, Frank Glover, Carrie Griffiths, Ray Harris, Gwen Kitchen, Margery Mercer, Mersey Valley Warden, Jean Peacock, Jim Pugh, Alex Royle, Bill Shercliff, Wylex Ltd.

Contents

Horse Bus leaving the Church Inn. *(left)*
The horse bus with its limited range continued to run on this route until 1909.

'Distance no object' *(below)*
Less limited range were the services advertised by A. W. Chantler in St. Wilfrid's Parish Magazine of the 1930s; although distance was no object we are not told whether the destination, up or down, had any bearing.

Introduction

Northenden today still has the spirit of a village – not a pretty chocolate box village but one that has learnt to adjust to changing times and a new environment without losing its identity.

The village is mentioned in the Domesday book but it is likely that there was a church here well before that time; because of the river and the ford, its origin probably goes back to very early times. For much of its history, apart from brief encounters with the effects of the Civil War, Bonnie Prince Charlie and the Boer War, the people of Northenden would have been chiefly concerned with sowing, harvesting and milling and with the ups and downs of life under the generally benevolent dominance of the Tatton family.

The building of Palatine Road and bridge in the 1860s let Northenden develop as a pleasant riverside centre attracting commuters and day trippers from Manchester, but the Mersey held back any mass invasion from the City. Between 1926 and 1931 however, the defences were breached and the province of Wythenshawe, designed as Britain's first municipal Garden City and in fact larger than many established cities, burst out south of Northenden. At this time Northenden also became the site of the first municipal airport. For a while the bridgehead served as the heart of the new estates but with the completion of the Wythenshawe Civic Centre, Northenden became again, in spirit at least, a village; a Civic Society was formed 'for those who care for our village'. The feeling was reinforced when motorways completely enclosed Northenden.

The History of Northenden up to 1926 has been detailed in Wythenshawe Volume I. Although widely acclaimed its high cost made the publication of Volume II, (which is complete in manuscript form,) a too hazardous speculation for the present. This picture volume has been arranged to take the reader mentally around the area, and where the mind meanders the feet or car could profitably follow.

The book draws on the researches of both volumes of *Wythenshawe* and it offers an outline history of the area as well as capturing some of the essence of the village that was, and is, Northenden.

A Den in the North, a Shaw of Willows and the Mersey

The River Mersey has always been a key feature of Northenden. The low banks of the flood plain gave easy access to the fertile wooded acres of Wythenshawe for Bronze and Stone Age man. The ford of Ford lane provided an early *saltway* for traders between the Cheshire saltfields and northern England as well as a route for a hard-pressed Bonnie Prince Charlie in 1745.

Many local place names stem from the river and the woodlands round Northenden. The Mersey – 'a mark, measure or boundary', formed the northern limit of the Kingdom of Mercia and later of Cheshire.

Relative to the river, Northenden was thus a Northern-'den' or dale. Sharston might have been a boundary Corner-stone or a stone by a wood or Shaw-stone, *shaw* still meaning a copse or wood today. (See page 38.)

Wythenshawe was a withy – willow, copse or shaw; other local woody names include Cringlewood, Hazel-hurst, (hurst-a hillock), Poundswick, (wick–an oak), Royal Thorn and Yew Tree. Baguley is a badger *lea* or *clearing* and similarly we have Kenworthy, Longley, Brownley and Haveley Hey. Etchells was an estate added later.

The river itself powered a mill for centuries and made a natural barrier to expanding Manchester until 1931. In the 19th century Northenden became a haven for tense Mancunians with boating, fairs, tea-houses and golf. Although pierced by pylons and motorways Northenden's Merseyside retains enough elegance to grace the new Mersey Valley park of the 1980s.

Northenden Weir and Mill shortly before demolition in the early 1960s.

In a deed of 1311 a selion or strip of land was granted to 'William the millar'. Two centuries later records show the Tattons of Wythenshawe Hall as the owners with the right to make all their tenants use the mill and pay a fee. The Tattons were a scion of the Lord Egerton family and the local landowners. A Tatton heir, William, drowned in the Mersey in 1617.

' Marooned Family Rescued from Floods by Rowing Boat '. *(left and inset)*
One item to reach the headlines of the national popular press was the rescue of Mr. and Mrs. Pegge and Baby John from Didsbury Golf Club in January 1932. ' Six policemen and others dragged and carried a boat half a mile. Nearly 10 feet of water surround the clubhouse. Mr. Price, his sons and other helpers, managed to put a ladder to the top window of the house and today they brought food and supplies.'

Flooding in Mill Lane, early 1970s. *(below)*
The problem of flooding persisted to recent times. In spite of major works by the River Authorities it seems some property was always to have the Mersey, the quality always unstrained. The building towards the right is the Gospel Hall which had a flourishing congregation in the earlier part of the century.

Boats waiting for visitors. *(below left)*
A small motor boat, for many years under the control of 'Old Bob', took visitors as far as Simon's Bridge and back.

Boathouse and boats on the Mersey about 1900.

Northenden became a venue for holiday trippers in the last century with boating as a big attraction. Cycling clubs, walkers, pony-traps, charabancs and gigs escaped from Manchester 'like a swarm of bees'. In the background is the Church with the Old Rectory and Rectory Cottage to the left and the Hollies, now the Rectory, to the right.

The Parish Church of St. Wilfrid

Crowning the top of a small hill that rises sharply from the river, St. Wilfrid's Church may have been founded before Northenden began.

Wilfrid was Bishop of Ripon in the 9th century and he worked successfully to establish the Roman Church in Britain. He travelled widely but we can only speculate that he visited the site of the church at Northenden.

The Domesday book of 1086 has the record, (translated), ' In Bucklow Hundred – Randle and Bigot hold of the Earl NORWORDINE. Ulvert held it as one manor and was a free man. There is one hide that pays geld. There is land for two ploughs. It is waste. There is a church and two furlongs of woodland. It is worth 3 shillings. It was worth ten shillings in the time of Edward the Confessor.'

After the defeat of Charles I, Thomas Mallory, the Rector of the time, was ejected and in the purge of idolatory the Parliamentary troops smashed the East window.

When rebuilding of the Church began in 1873 the foundations of earlier structures were found. Some of the Old Rectory adjoining the Church was built in the early 18th century and the foundations are those of an earlier building.

Pencil Drawing of Northenden Old Church. Over three or more centuries the church was rebuilt and restored many times. By 1870, however, it was dangerous and it was decided to erect a new structure, keeping only the tower. The eminent Victorian architect Joseph Crowther, who restored Manchester Cathedral, was chosen for the work. Behind the church on the right is the 1840 Infants' School-cum-temporary-church.

Sundial by the old church. *(above)*
The rebuilding was dogged by strikes and at one point a side roof collapsed. In addition to the tower there has been retained from the old church an ancient screen, 'the handsomest in Cheshire', an early font dug up in the Rectory Gardens and the sundial, now behind railings.

Maids of the Rectory outside the Conservatory, 1873. *(above right)*
The enlarged rectory of the 19th century needed a housekeeper, four maids, butler, groom gardener and stable boy. The larger halls and houses needed many times this number and a good proportion of the population in the area was 'in service' at this time.

' The Rectory Servants and Bruce', 1873. *(right)*
The photograph was taken inside the conservatory which was taken down in the mid 1950s.

Aerial Photograph of the Church, 1926.
Crowther's new church was built in the style of the old, but about six feet higher. At this time the churchyard was levelled and extended. The earliest grave is dated 1596 and the stone of Henry Dunster, a dissenting minister of the Commonwealth period and 'lately a most vigorous pastor of this church' is near the East window. The 15th century tower was restored at about the time that this picture was taken.

Victorian addition to the old rectory.

The earliest part of the old rectory is the early Georgian three storey building that faces the church. The two storey early Victorian wing with the lantern-end was made to match in height the earlier part. In the last century its kitchens, stables and conservatory covered twice the area of building left today. Of these additions only the stables remain and they are in use as Rectory Cottage.

On the (old) rectory lawn the young Fred Perry, future world champion, practised tennis when visiting Rector Hamilton's brother who was himself a Wimbledon player.

Church Garden Party, about 1972.
Instituted in the 1880s the garden parties were revived in the 1960s, often with maypole dancing from St. Wilfrid's school, and Northenden Silver Prize Band which had started off as a church venture in the 1930s.

Tea Stall at St. Wilfrid's garden party, late 1960s. *(far left)*
Centre, serving without a hat, is Miss Ethel Price whose family took part in the flood rescue recounted in the first section.

Choir of St. Wilfrid's and Mr. Sockett. *(above)*
The post Second World War period was a boom time for St. Wilfrid's Church. The organ was rebuilt in the west end, where it had been earlier, in 1963.

Rev. Sockett and Wardens, late 1950s. *(left)*
Some of the practices such as Whit Walks which were brought from the inner city to the new Wythenshawe churches, were taken up for a time by the established churches. The walk is here moving along Palatine Road shortly after leaving the Mersey bridge.

Ford Lane

The ancient *saltway* of Ford Lane, after passing the church and rectory, leads to the river and the ford. At the upper end, near the church, grew a community of houses and cottages.

The lane was for centuries the most direct, if damp, route to Manchester and in time the Boat Lane turning by the church led to a ferry. The present girder bridge on Palatine Road was built in 1884 when Northenden was growing as a dormitory suburb for Manchester, and it replaced a footbridge of twenty years earlier.

On Lampits Lane half way down the hill, can be traced the village pond. Opposite this and parallel to the river the plan of medieval strip farming can be discerned in the area, called Swineworth or Sun Earth. Appropriately this is still used for allotments today.

Where the lane joins the river, now a caravan park, was once, (beside the boathouse and the fair,) a stadium. Before being burnt down in 1962 it had been used for roller skating, concerts, boxing and as an amusement arcade.

Ford Lane, facing east. *(left)*
The cottages on the right were demolished about 1900 and replaced by Price's wood-yard, the upper rooms of the building being used by the Dramatic Society. It was itself replaced by the Church Rooms in 1965.

The cottage behind the finger post is known as Cromwell Cottage because the Roundhead troops probably stabled their horses there when they purged the Church.

'Northenden Village'; Ford Lane *(above)*
This post card was posted by a Scout to his father in Ireland in 1915. It shows Ford Lane where it passes the Church at the highest point in Northenden, before dropping down to the river. The finger post pointing down Boat Lane is marked 'To Manchester'.

Ford Lane facing west with Northen House on the right. *(right)*

Northen House was once owned by Lord Egerton. It forms with the Old Rectory and the Church a trio of listed buildings in the Northenden Conservation Area.

Troops resting in Ford Lane – 'W.T.' College Training 1914. *(below right)*

Although leading in the Manchester direction from Northenden, the lane has long provided country walks for locals: the troops probably had other thoughts. The Tatton Arms footbridge at Northenden and the Simon's footbridge (which fell in the river during erection,) at Didsbury, give access to the other bank.

Air Raid Wardens for the Ford Lane Area, about 1942. *(below)*

The photograph was taken in Ford Lane on the land that is now the Village Green. 'I suppose we got off fairly lightly' was the overall verdict, though the Mill Lane toilets and a cottage within the domain of these wardens, opposite Patterdale Road, were hit. The wardens include Mrs. Naylor and Mr. Naylor seated, Mr. Bunn, Mr. Proctor and two district wardens.

Ford Lane, Church Inn and Church Road, about 1925.
The top end of Ford Lane, known for a time as Church Street, is in the foreground with Price's wood-yard to the left.

Ford Lane, Church Inn and Church Road nearly fifty years later.
This scene is also taken from the Church tower. Price's wood-yard has gone and the air is cleaner. Superficially little has changed but the corner house and the cottages were later demolished. On the corner a village green was created and opposite a police station was planned.

Local Hostelries.

Within 200 metres of the Church are five of Northenden's public houses. The Spread Eagle and the Jolly Carter were rebuilt in the 1960s and 1970s respectively. The Tatton Arms and the Church Inn were rebuilt in the late 19th century leaving the Crown as the oldest, and smallest, alehouse.

The Farmers Arms in Longley Lane served the outlying hamlet at Moor End. Further in the same direction is Northenden's newest and grandest pub, the Post House which commands extensive views of the Motorway! (See page 44.) Today licences are also held by the British Legion and the Northenden Social Club.

The Church Inn and the Spread Eagle before the erection of the 1897 building. *(above)*

The Church Inn, about 1935. *(left)*
The Village Green has generally been associated with the area to the front of the Church Inn at the junction of Church Road, Ford Lane and Royle Green Road. It has in times past been the site for a maypole, bear baiting and pottery stalls. The present Church Inn dates from 1897 and is in a style reminiscent of American saloons of the same period.

Motor Bus at the Church Inn about 1910. *(opposite)*
After earlier trials motor buses ran from the Church Inn to Manchester from 1909. They were at first noted for 'unreliability, . . . breakdowns and inconvenient times of running'.

The Spread Eagle in the early 1960s.
These are two of many photographs by John Hill-Wilson who set out to record Northenden before its character was lost. The Royle Green Flats have already appeared in the distance.

The Crown Inn, about 1970.
Taken from the Church Tower the photograph shows the Crown, often called the Corner Pin, before all the adjoining houses were demolished in 1978. The area at the top is at the rear of the Church Inn where it is said bear-baiting once took place. It was from one of the stables there that the body of Cotterhill, the Bradley Gate murderer, was taken by a mob and kicked down the street. (See account on page 43.)

The Jolly Carter in the 1960s.
It was at this time still two converted cottages.
Cock fighting is said to have taken place here in
an upper room.

The Jolly Carter Bowling Club. *(inset)*
This is one of a number of photographs by
Mr. Warren, (see the Church Road section page
24) taken about 1905 and loaned by Mr. Saul.

The Farmers' Arms. *(below)*

This appears to be another example of cottages converted in the early 19th century. In 1911 the owner, Peter Leigh, built what soon became the Coronation Cinema, on an adjacent site. In the many intervals patrons could complement their mental refreshment with liquid replenishment.

(Inset) **Farmers' Arms customers at the turn of the century.**

The Boathouse Inn about 1860. *(below right)*

The ferry was worked by ropes and continued in use until the footbridge was erected in the 1870s.

The Tatton Arms in the 1930s.

The structure of 1875 replaced the ancient Boat House Inn that formerly profited from the ferry and later from the fairs and boating. (See page 1.)

Church Road and a new Village Centre.

Before the creation of Palatine Road in 1861 Church Road was the main road in and through Northenden. As the village grew in the 19th century the junction of Church Road, Kenworthy Lane and Palatine Road became a new village centre.

The Junction of Church Road and Palatine Road in the 1890s.

The Post Office run by Nields is on the right. The photograph would have been taken from the site of the future Church School which is itself now replaced, from the 1960s, by Tesco's Supermarket.

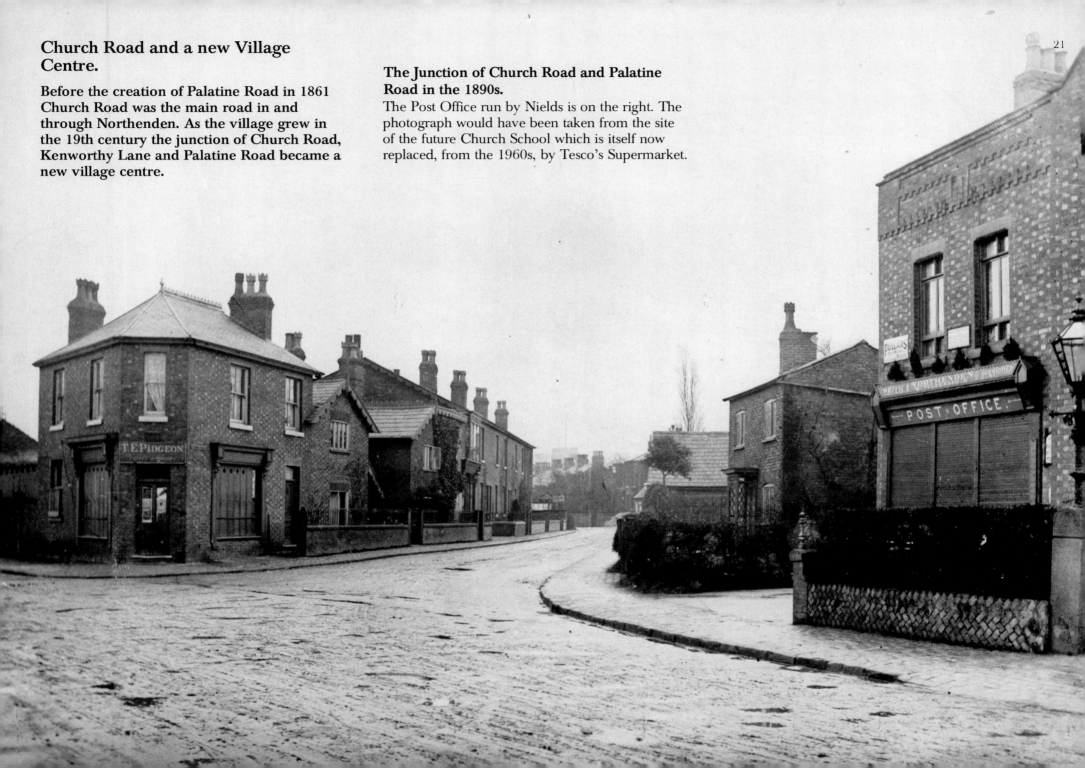

The Church Inn from Church Road about 1900.

There are still vestiges of a green belt between the old village green area in this picture and the new trading centre at the Palatine end of Church Road. The building on the right is the Working Men's Club of 1866: facilities included a reading room and talks given included 'The History of Northenden' and 'Sewage and Water Pollution'. Later the building became a library, a centre for the school meals and today is a dancing school.

The Church Inn from Church Road in the 1960s. *(left)*

The corner shop to the left is at present a laundrette but was earlier the first premises of the District Bank. A one-time manager of the Bank, Arthur Royle, was a general factotum of Northenden and local historian. His father had been headmaster of Sharston School.

A Card from the Arthur Royle Collection.*(right)*
These pictures and notes on his own bank are
from the Arthur Royle Collection about
Northenden and are at present in Wythenshawe
Library. The notes read: 'Mr. Royle, the
Manager, outside the bank which was opened
March 1930 in Church Road and enlarged 1940.
Mr. Royle retired in 1955. The First Branch was
in 1919 in the shop which is now a Laund . . .'
(sic).

**Coxell and Co., Grocers, Church Road about
1900.***(below)*
On the extreme left, opposite the Church Inn is
the Oddfellows' Hall.

Warren's Cash Drug Store.

This is the third of the new Church Road Shops; the proprietor was responsible for many of the photographs of the early 1900s. Notice the claim of 'Teeth Carefully Extracted' and the coupons with Bovril.

The middle stretch of Church Road, early 1900s.

The backdrop is the Church Inn and to its left are farm buildings and Ravenswood Terrace of 1901. This replaced 'Ravenswood' which was once the home of Joseph Johnson, a Radical who by involving Henry Hunt had effectively set the scene for the Peterloo massacre of 1820. The gate to the right is to the Cedars farm. On the extreme left are the end two of four smart new shops.

Mr. Warren's shop in the 1950's. *(inset)*
The Cash Drug Store is by now a café.

'Jack'. The Rector's pony in 1883.

Mr. Warren's Photographs. *(below)*

Flower's Milk Cart and Hamer's of Rusholme Bakery Van.

Advertisements of local traders at that time stressed the cleanliness of Northenden compared with Manchester: 'Don't eat soot – buy your bread locally' said one advert in the Parish magazine.

Rose Cottages.
Built in 1701 they were in seemingly good
condition when Mr. Warren had them
photographed at the beginning of this century.

**The Cedars and Rose Cottages in the early
1960s.**
The Cedars had become Herbert Brunt's dairy. A
caravan library was to be parked on the site of the
Rose cottages for nearly twenty years before a
proper library was built in 1982. The Post Office
had earlier been at the shop on the opposite
corner, Pidgeons, with a private school above.

Churches and Schools round the new Centre.

It was to the region centred on the junction of Church Road and Palatine Road rather than the Parish Church that new churches and schools, as well as houses and shops, were attracted at the end of the last century.

The Methodists built their first chapel, nine metres square, in 1828. Their present church was started in 1876 behind the earlier one and it was enlarged in 1908.

The Catholics, who had had to leave St. Wilfrid's building at the time of the Reformation, re-opened for business in 1904 in, appropriately enough, an ex-Protestant church.

A Gospel Hall opposite the mill flourished for half a century from its inception in 1887 but is now a timber store. The Quakers have a meeting house on Wythenshawe Road. The Jehovah's Witnesses took over the old Forum Cinema in 1977 (see page 34) and the Mormons have a large church on Altrincham Road.

The only school in Northenden until the 1900s had been one for Infants in Ford Lane. The school at Sharston – more central to the whole parish, was dated 1869 and was the third on the site. There were also schools at Baguley and at Shadow Moss where the building also served as a church.

A new Church of England School was built at the new village centre opposite the Post Office in 1901. It stayed until the present school was erected in Patterdale Road. A Methodist School appeared in the same year and was used until the Council School was built in Bazley Road a few years later.

St. Wilfrid's Church School, the 'National School', about 1903. *(Inset)*
The School and the Church Rooms at the rear (1913) were to be at the centre of an increasingly busy Northenden for the next half century. The Church Rooms were the venue for most village events as well as the momentous meeting concerned with the move of Wythenshawe into Manchester.

Sharston Tea Rooms, formerly Sharston School. *(above)*
Auctioned off when the Northenden Church School opened in 1901 it flourished as Tea Rooms with tourist and local trade until replaced by the Sharston Hotel in the late 1930s.

Church School, Boys, about 1950. *(inset left)*
This is a unique photograph as the boys were forbidden to enter the girl's playground where this was taken!

Church School Pageant, 1960.

Mrs. Griffiths' Class with Maypole, 1964. *(inset right)*

Rev. Chignell with scholars passing the Crescent Studios on Palatine Road, opposite Lingard Road, about 1935. *(left)*

Miss Price and Councillor Walmsley with St. Wilfrid's Church members on the way to the turf cutting ceremony of the proposed new school. *(below)*

The Palatine Road School was replaced by a school on Patterdale Road in 1960 and eventually Tesco's supermarket appeared on the old site.

Kenworthy Lane, Northenden, 1902.*(below left)*

Only a few yards past the side of the Church School were these country lanes. In the late 1920s the 'first 142' Manchester Council houses (see page 39) were sited here while Northenden was still in Cheshire. Notice the baby carriage at the point where Yew Tree Lane branches off.

St. Hilda's Roman Catholic Church, Kenworthy Lane. *(top left)*

The building was erected as a private chapel by Mrs. Ziba Ward of Cringlewood. It opened as a Protestant place of worship in 1901 but with little effect and so was sold to the Catholics in 1904; they used it for the next seventy years when it was replaced by a structure in the style of the Liverpool R.C. Cathedral.

(top right)

The Methodist Church, 1955, front entrance.
The present building dates from 1876 and an
enlargement from 1908. The large tree in the
foreground, one of the last vestiges of the country
in this part of Northenden, was removed in 1965
to make way for a bus lay-by.

The Methodist School of 1901. *(above)*
It was built at the same time as the Palatine Road
Church of England School but when the Council
School opened a few years later the staff were
moved across. The building was eventually
replaced by a Youth Centre.

'Northenden Council School, 1907.' *(right)*
The new school in Bazley Road had 400 places
and 'facilities for the teaching of cookery, laundry,
housewifery and manual instruction'.

Northenden Council School Staff about 1930.
In time the separate buildings at the front were
taken over as dental and medical clinics. *(far right)*

Leisure and Pleasure

Many of the Northenden churches and schools were involved in social and leisure activities. Sometimes, as with the band and the drama and football groups, these developed into separate bodies; often entertainment, education and exercise overlapped. Some organisations such as the Rosemary Fund were started by traders, and others by pubs, clubs and commercial concerns. In a community practised in the art of self-help, a number of organisations and events such as the Literary Societies sprang up spontaneously, or to mark special occasions.

Northenden Social Club, Executive Committee, Second World War. *(above)*
Formed as the Northenden Comrades of the Great War Club after the First World War it moved into new premises in 1926 and twelve years later became Northenden Social Club.

British Legion officials outside the Spread Eagle. *(left)*
A branch was not formed in Northenden until 1958 when Wythenshawe's branch was thirty years old. By 1964 however, on the site of Turner's Coal-yard in Royle Green Road, opposite the Spread Eagle, they had established a thriving club.

Messrs Walters and Levy's Summer *(above)*
Entertainers – The Marguerite Quartette.
One of Mr. Warren's photographs, it was
probably taken on the river bank about 1905; if
this is so it is likely that the troupe was performing
at the Stadium in Ford Lane.

Amateur Dramatics – NADS. *(top right)*
After a successful performance of A Midsummer
Night's Dream on the rectory lawn, the NADS –
Northenden Amateur Dramatic Society was
formed in 1921 and normally played in the
Church Rooms, Kenworthy Lane. In 1939 it
reached the finals in London of the News
Chronicle Amateur Dramatic Contest. In the
Second World War the remaining players formed
the Younger Generation; after the war they took
over from the NADS and eventually became the
Northenden Players.

Northenden Public Subscription Band, 1951.
(below right)
The band began as a Church sponsored venture in
1929 but it became independent a few years later
and in time became the Northenden Silver Prize
Band. The setting of the photograph is the bowling
green of the Northenden Social Club and in the
background may be seen the Club's tennis courts
and the new telephone exchange.

Forum Cinema, Wythenshawe Road, Rin-Tin-Tin showing. *(left)*
The cinema opened in 1934 and had a fine Wurlitzer organ and restaurant, and was also equipped for stage shows. On Hollyhedge Road, Wythenshawe was due to have its own cinema in 1939: the Council wanted an £18,000 palace but ABC were only prepared to spend £14,000 when the war intervened.

Former Forum Cinema – Kingdom Hall. *(below left)*
The Jehovah's Witnesses restored the former splendour in 1976 though Burton-on-Trent had the Wurlitzer Organ and the Wythenshawe complex had taken the name Forum.

The one-time Coronation Cinema, Longley Lane, 1969. *(below)*
Peter Leigh, owner of the adjacent Farmers' Arms, built the hall in 1911 then quickly adapted it as a cinema. It had bentwood cane chairs, its own electric generator, pictures on a white-washed wall and liquid refreshment on tap. It became a Bingo Hall in 1964.

Young Wives Keep Fit Class 1935. *(above)*
The picture by Mrs. Bunn was taken at Beech
House on Yew Tree Lane. This was once the
home of a Thomas Lings, a leading market
gardener; it was owned later by Robert Percival, a
wealthy property owner who in 1877 presented
the Church with an organ. In the First World War
it was used as a hospital and eventually as a centre
for district nurses and a clinic. On the left of the
picture is an arch moved from Manchester
Cathedral during restoration work.

Rosemary Festival 1938. *(middle right)*
The Fund was set up by the Rotary Club and
traders in 1934 and over the next thirty years
raised huge sums for charity as well as providing
colourful spectacles in the process.

**St. Wilfrid's Social and Athletic Club – Burton
Cup Team 1938–9.** *(above right)*
The Club was an amalgamation of two groups that
had been formed in 1927. Supported by the
profits of concerts, dances and other social events,
the team was runner-up in the Wythenshawe and
District Amateur Football League of 1939.

**Northenden Literary Society Membership
Card, 1933–4.** *(right)*
The meetings were at the Church Rooms on
Wednesdays at 8 p.m. The Society began in 1899
and in that year talks were given on Gladstone
and Socialism.

OFFICER OF THE SOCIETY
1933-34.

President : Mr. W. KENNEDY.

Vice-President : Miss F. LEES.

Past President : Mr. R. ATHERTON.

Committee :

Mrs. J. Watson.
Mrs. W. Kennedy.
Mrs. E. Voce.
Mr. W. B. Buckley.
Mr. R. S. Clark.
Mr. M. R. Davies.

Mr. W. R. Hey.
Mr. W. Plant.
Mr. F. Sergeant.
Mr. E. C. Tomlinson.
Mr. J. Watson.
Mr. W. Wolstenholme.

Hon. Treasurer : Mr. L. M. Davies, B.A.,
Kenworthy Lane, Northenden.

Hon. Lanternist : Mr. E. G. Woodhouse.

Hon. Auditor : Mr. L. M. S. Scotter.

Joint Hon Secretaries :
Mr. A. J. G. Watson.
"Kennedy," Kenworthy Lane, Northenden.
Mr. R. Atherton, 2, Beech Avenue, Northenden.

ANNUAL SUBSCRIPTION 1/6

Northenden
Literary Society

Membership Ticket
AND
Syllabus
TWENTY-SEVENTH SESSION
1933-34

'Northenden Volunteer Fire Brigade'. *(above)*
Convincing, but in fact a float at the pageant to mark Victoria's Diamond Jubilee at Rosehill in 1897. Records indicate that Northenden at this time had to use the brigade from Sale and Ashton Joint Service. Upon the incorporation of Northenden into Manchester in 1931 the city brigade took over the responsibility that they had in practice been providing for the previous decade.

Fancy Dress Ball, Church Rooms, probably 1937. *(top left)*
It is thought that the ball was held to mark the coronation of George VI. Walter Raleigh was portrayed by Jim Pugh, later to be a founder member of the Civic Society. Centre blacked-up is Elsie Walmsley, later a Councillor. Seated right is Mrs. Hewlett whose husband had a decade earlier firmly opposed the incorporation of Wythenshawe into Manchester at a bitter meeting in this room; their son became a television actor who starred in 'It Ain't Half Hot, Mum'.

Methodist Youth Centre, Victoria Road nearing completion in 1971. *(above)*
The new centre was on the site of the old Methodist School. It was largely financed by the Education Committee but the long term arrangements for supervision ran into difficulties. On the left is the Methodist Church Hall of 1954.

General Bulmer and Aide. *(far left)*
These are two other characters represented at the Diamond Jubilee pageant. There was another Grand Pageant in Wythenshawe Park in 1926 to mark the presentation of the Hall and Park by Ernest Simon to the public. Colonel Duckenfield was played by Arthur Royle.

Village into Country.

Apart from organised activities, probably the healthiest pursuit of Northenden villagers well into the present century, was the enjoyment of the surrounding Cheshire countryside. Walks abounded, and dotted over the scene were the stately homes of the gentry, the farmers and the nouveau riche. The Lord of the Manor, the local Squire, came from the Tatton family of Wythenshawe Hall.

This peaceful picture could not last. A few miles to the north, Manchester with its slums was clamouring for living room. In 1919 Professor Abercrombie was asked to look for a site; he reported that the Wythenshawe area was 'eminently suitable for a Housing Scheme'. In just over a dozen years the first council-house tenants, chosen very carefully at first, would be experiencing the affectious spirit of the harvest fly at first hand – and leg.

Wythenshawe Hall, 1959. *(below)*
The Tattons first had land in Northenden in the 13th century and they became full Lords of the

Manor in the 16th century when the present hall was started. In the Civil War it was beseiged by the army of Cromwell whose statue graces the front. The much extended and expensively restored half timber hall has 17th century furniture, Royal Lancastrian pottery prints and interesting relics. When the Tattons at last agreed to sell the Wythenshawe estates in 1926, Ernest Simon gave the hall and grounds to Manchester.

Restoration work in 1983 uncovered a 400 years old wall painting of a Bacchus-like figure and workmen's graffiti from the same period.

Sharston Hall about 1900. *(inset)*
Once described as 'the best house of the date in Manchester', this 18th century Hall was long in the hands of the Worthington family, some of whose money came from the manufacture of umbrellas. Thomas Worthington led the Troop against the Chartist rioters in Stockport. In the 1920s the Hall belonged to the Henriques family but it was converted into flats after they were involved in a tragic motor accident. In the Second World War it became headquarters of the police, civil defence and fire services; since then it has been in want of someone with a genuine interest in a fine old hall.

Rose Hill, about 1950. *(right)*

Sir Edward Watkins, a railway magnate in Britain and Canada, had the huge stone brought to his 19th century mansion late in the last century by horses and cart. Miss Southern of Sharston Mount, believes the stone was the boundary or 'shar' stone, of Sharston. The house became a Children's Hospital and later a Remand Home. In 1981 a painting of Icebergs by Church was 'discovered' and at £3M became the fifth highest priced painting in the world at the time. As the frame was engraved 'to the people of Northenden in perpetuity' it became the subject of litigation.

(inset) **The Icebergs.**

Harvest Festival, St. Wilfrid's 1942. *(below)*

The Harvest Festival marked the completion of a critically important job in the farmer's year. At St. Wilfrid's, in spite of the war the time was still well observed and the spirit of the countryside prevailed. The black-out curtains were borrowed from the Dramatic Society.

Country into Town.

Following the Abercrombie Report, Manchester in 1926 bought the Wythenshawe estates. After heated meetings in the Church Rooms and elsewhere the Cheshire landowners persuaded Parliament to refuse the incorporation of the land into the City and control of the area remained with Bucklow Council at Knutsford.

In five years of fillibustering the Council gave permission for only 142 houses to be built when Manchester needed 50,000. The '142' erected in Kenworthy Lane, became a battle symbol. Prodded by William Jackson, Ernest Simon and Lt. Col. Westcott, the Wythenshawe Committee was formed and it engaged the foremost town planner of the day, Barry Parker. Impressed by his scheme Parliament allowed Manchester to acquire the area and Parker was free to put into effect his plan for Wythenshawe as the first full-scale Garden City in Britain.

Henly's Garage, Princess Parkway – Wythenshawe Road junction, about 1940.
From the overall plan to details of house design, Barry Parker took charge but he especially recognised the need for good attractive motor links and for separate service roads.

Barry Parker (inset)

Benchill and Royal Oak Times, 1934. *(right)*
Ten Neighbourhood units, each with its own shops and schools to serve about 10,000 people were planned by Barry Parker. The Benchill and Royal Oak Times, run from 325 Altrincham Road, ominously warned readers not to trust their panel (doctor's) prescriptions to unknown canvassers.

Petal Throwers, Rosemary Festival at Yew Tree School, 1938. *(below)*
Yew Tree School, built to serve the Northenden and Rackhouse area, was the first Neighbourhood School in Wythenshawe in 1934. It became Manchester's first Comprehensive School and in 1982 a Sixth Form College. The Festival was an important money raising event for the local charity that began in the early 1930s.

Bridge Construction, 1927. *(above top)*
The Princess Road Bridge was the first task undertaken in the Wythenshawe scheme.

Princess Road Bridge, 1960. *(above)*
After forty years of gracing Princess Parkway this unpretentious dignified bridge was submerged with motorway concrete.

Civic Week installation ceremony in Wythenshawe Park, 1957. *(right)*

The Recorder, (later the Express,) began in 1937 in Northenden as a free paper. It campaigned for Civic Weeks and for self-government for Wythenshawe whose population, it noted, was twice that of Chester and equalled Cambridge. It also kept up a running feud in the correspondence columns between Wythenshawe and Northenden.

Wylex and other factories with Northenden station, 1935. *(below)*

Barry Parker planned that two of the Industrial Estates, Sharston and Royal Thorn, should be served by the existing rail links. Freight traffic boomed and Northenden passenger station was popular for excursions but for daily use it was too far from the village and the route to Manchester too circuitous. When it closed in 1965 the local paper reported that 'most people thought it had closed years ago'.

Northenden Junction, bridge and signal box, about 1955. *(below right)*

Into the Future.

Caught between ageing Manchester and an adolescent Wythenshawe, turmoil and change were inevitable for Northenden. For a time the village profited as a shopping and cultural heart for the fledgling estates. A Civic Society was formed to resist a monorail that would have split the village; but a few years later it could not hold back the motorways that would surround the community. Added to this the garden city was beginning to sprout, and the new Civic Centre drew over many traders and services.

In detachment Northenden again had the feel of a village; the village green was revived, the older half of the village was made a Conservation Area and as part of the restoration of the Mersey Valley, Northenden's river retrieved some of its ancient dignity.

'Please Stop Dropping Litter', Palatine Road, about 1960.
To the left is the Moor End parade of shops, the first in Parker's plan. The Church of England School behind the trees, and Barrow Motors converted barn, centre, were still intact. Vibrations of the banner broke the lamp on the right. The constabulary arrived to remove the litter, and so did John Hill Wilson with camera.

Bradley Gate, Longley Lane, opposite the present Royle Green Garage.*(above)*
The area is being cleared for Council Houses, chiefly for residents from Hulme, 1959.

(above right) The funeral in 1902 at Bradley Gate of John Dyson who was murdered by his ex-butler. The murderer Cotterill shot at the police before being shot himself. Thought to have been pro-Boer and therefore nicknamed Kruger, his body was kicked along the road from the Church Inn. He is said to be buried in the churchyard behind the pillar box, (one of the few remaining marked VR,) in an unmarked grave. (See also page 18.)

Princess Mansions from under Princess Parkway, 1970.*(right)*
Princess Parkway, the grand link between Manchester and Wythenshawe in Parker's plan, is being upgraded to motorway standard and at this point it is being bridged over Wythenshawe Road. Princess Mansions, on the left, built in the early 1930s as luxury flats, were replaced in 1971 by the Post House Hotel.

A double decker bus collision opposite the Post House, 1979.
Eleven people were injured when the bus and a fire engine collided, the bus ending across a subway. The result was caught by Guardian photographer Denis Thorpe but the graffiti, a sympton of the unsavoury behaviour for which the subways became noted, was edited out before publication.

Mersey and motorway in conflict, 1972.
The motorway, part of the M63, ran along the Mersey Valley. This was the third local motorway and the three together enclosed the village: Northenden was striangulated.

Palatine Road, facing Manchester, 1954.
Heyridge Drive is just off the left side of the picture.

Palatine Road from the same spot 1955. *(inset)*
The New Parade which included Woolworth, Timothy Whites and Boots, was going up. The new shops helped Northenden to remain the middle level shopping centre for Wythenshawe but as the Civic Centre grew in the late 1960s trade in Northenden decreased. Of the three shops named, only Woolworth was still there by the 1980s.

Princess Parkway 1930 and 1958.
The Parks Department has made great efforts to restore to the motorway-style road the trees and shrubs that were the glory of the original road.

The Village Green in the course of being re-created, 1983. *(above)*
In the background is the Church-rooms of the mid-1960s. The picture makes an interesting comparison with other photographs here and in the Ford Lane section.

Shortlisted cottages Royle Green Road, 1970.
The two cottages which faced the Spread Eagle must hold the record as Listed Buildings with the shortest survival time. Found to have been of unique medieval crook construction they were listed for preservation early in 1982 and demolished the following morning.

Moor End Forge, Longley Lane. *(right)*
Northenden's last smithy was demolished in the early 1970s along with the police station which stood behind it.

Palatine Road, late 1950s. *(above)*
Barrow Motor's former building can be seen to the left; to the right of the crossing stands the Church School, blissfully unaware of the plans for a supermarket that would shortly take its place.

A.E. Smith and Co., Grocers, early 1960s.
On the corner of Brett Street this was one of the many shops converted from houses that would begin to make Palatine Road the main shopping centre in this century.